KT-171-816

The Art of Flower Arranging

Simple and Stylish Designs

APPLE

Northamptonshire
Libraries & Information
Service
ND

Askews & Holts

Acknowledgements

Thanks to Chris, Dané & Alwyn for generously allowing us to use Okasie as a photo studio, and making available all your flowerrs and containers. You taught me just about everything I know about flowers and flower arranging.
www.okasie.co.za +27 21 887 9904

Susan van Rensburg of "Perfect Place – fine food & coffee" (66 Church Street, Wellington, + 27 21 873 6620), Ouma Breda Rossouw, Carin Scheepers, Rod le Roux, Marié-Lise Coetzee and Sandra Vorster for your containers.

First published in the United Kingdom in 2010
by Apple Press
7 Greenland Street
London NW1 9EE
www.apple-press.com

Copyright © Metz Press 2009
Text and designs copyright © Ansia Kohrs
Photographs copyright © Metz Press

All rights reserved. No part of this publication may be reproduced, stored in a retrieval system or transmitted in any form or by any means, electronic, mechanical, photocopying, recording or otherwise, without the prior written permission of the copyright owners.

Publisher	Wilsia Metz
Design and lay-out	Lindie Metz
Translation	Lesley Howard
Photographer	Ivan Naudé
Assistant	Rowina Keiller
Colour wheel	Nikki Miles
Reproduction	Color/Fuzion

Printed and bound in China
by WKT Company Ltd
ISBN 978-1-84543-374-1

Contents

Introduction

Flowers have a much greater impact on us than we imagine – from a stolen daisy to a bunch of the most expensive roses. Without words flowers tell us: "I am thinking of you"; "I love you". Flowers beautify and brighten our lives.

Until quite recently there were strict rules that applied to the arrangement of flowers. For many years flower arrangements were stiff and stilted, and one did not dare to use a container that was not in exact proportion to the flowers. Although some rules will always have a place when it comes to flower arranging, free arrangements are much more the vogue today. Flower arranging is after all just another medium in which one can express one's creativity. Step-by-step this book will show you a few useful techniques and hints on how to make your flowers last longer in the arrangement. May these guidelines inspire original creations of your own.

Before you begin

Having the correct tools
and containers will make
the creation of your
arrangement easier
and a pleasure.

Secateurs
Ideal for cutting
hardwood stems. also the
softer green stems. Ensure that
your secateurs are sharp so that
you do not damage the plant material.

Scissors
Use ordinary domestic scissors for the
cutting of leaves and finer stems; also for
cutting ribbon and fine wire.

Knife
For the cutting of stems and oases.

Rose stripper

Useful for stripping the thorns from a rose. It is not an essential tool, as you can snip each thorn off the stem using a knife or a pair of small secateurs, but using a rose stripper will make your task much easier. Start just under the leaf that you want to keep, squeeze the stripper lightly and pull it gently downwards from the bloom. If you work too roughly the stem breaks off easily.

Feathers/beads

To add another dimension to your arrangement, fasten feathers or beads on the tips of florist's wire.

Ribbon/lace

This is useful for finishing a bunch of flowers to be used as a gift, but it can also be used as part of the arrangement.

Wire

Wire of different thicknesses and lengths is always handy. It can be used for the support of hollow-stemmed flowers in large arrangements and for the creation of wreaths and posies. Fine gold, silver, bronze or copper wire can be used for decoration.

String/raffia

Use to bind bunches of flowers or posies.

Florist's adhesive tape

This is used when necessary to finish off wired flowers.

Filament tape

This is stronger than normal adhesive tape and is useful for holding oasis in place, or to form a grid over a container with a large mouth that will hold the flowers in the position you desire.

Tissue paper

Works well to finish off a gift arrangement.

Flower food (in gel or crystal form)

Not an essential, but placed in the water of the arrangement they serve not only as plant food, but also keep the water clear and clean as they contain anti-bacterial agents. You can also use them in the water that wets the oasis.

Household containers

It is useful to have a variety of containers to hand. Quite often your desired containers, such as baskets, will not be watertight. It is not always necessary to buy special containers. Used margarine or yoghurt tubs can work just as well, but always ensure that they do not show once the arrangement is in place.

Buckets

Place the flowers for the arrangement in a bucket full of water before you begin.

Watering cans

A can with a narrow spout makes the watering of arrangements so much easier, but if you do not have one, a cool drink bottle will work just as well.

Refillable spray cans

Ideal for spraying your arrangement with water. This will keep the blooms fresh and cool.

Dodder

This is a parasitic climber that grows on a variety of other plants. The flexible stems of dodder are ideal for finishing arrangements off and for creating interesting shapes.

Gel crystals

Gel crystals are water absorbing polymers. They were originally developed to improve water retention in soil, especially in dry areas or areas where there is rapid water run-off. These crystals expand when water is added to them, and contract with evaporation. They are able to expand once more when water is added again. In flower arrangements they serve not only as a source of water, but also add an interesting effect and help to support the flower stems.

Oasis

Oasis™ is the trade name for the spongy phenolic foam that is used for flower arranging. It is usually green in colour, but is available in other colours at selected florist shops. It draws water like a sponge and then acts as a source of water, an oasis so to speak, for the flowers in the arrangement. It also serves to hold the flowers in position. These days it is readily available in a variety of forms and colours, and indeed makes the arranging of flowers much easier.

The use of oasis comes naturally to some people, but there are 'rules' to be followed in its use. After a number of experiments and advice from those in the know, I am able to share the following tips with you:

- Always cut the oasis slightly larger than the container into which it must fit. This ensures that the oasis fits snugly and does not move around in the container.
- Do not make the oasis too big, as in the first place it will be difficult to fit into the container, and then when the foam compacts, it will also be difficult to push the stems into it. In addition, the movement of the water will impact on the condition of the flowers.
- Use a deep container or wash basin which is at least twice the depth of the oasis. Fill it with water and place the oasis in it. Do not force the oasis under the water. Allow the oasis to soak up water gradually. It will take a while, so be patient. Air bubbles will form if you force the oasis. Then when you arrange the flowers, the blooms will come in contact with the air bubbles and wilt.

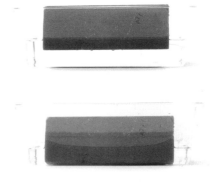

Oasis was traditionally completely covered with plant material, but these days it forms part of the arrangement, especially when the oasis is attractively coloured. For large arrangements use wire netting to strengthen the oasis. Used oasis that does not have too many holes in it can be employed again. It will not soak up the water as well as new oasis does. Place in boiling water rather than cold water as described above and follow the same method. Ensure that the oasis and the water have cooled down completely before you begin so that the flowers are not damaged.

Containers and vases

To begin with, four or five flower pots of
different shapes and sizes will be sufficient
for your creations. Once you are at home
and confident in flower arranging, you will
see potential in almost any container. A
pretty mayonnaise or jam jar, ink pots, your
grandmothers' old teapots, tea cups, milk
jugs, wine bottles, iron pots, grandpa's old
milk can (even if it is rusty and holed), even
the basket you wanted to throw out almost
two years ago – all of them can be used
as containers for flower arrangements. Do
not be put off by a small hole or two in a
container or the fear that it will be ruined.
Simply line the container with plastic or
place another watertight vessel inside it.

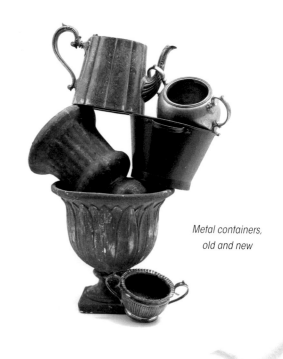

*Metal containers,
old and new*

*Pewter, silver, wood and
glazed ceramics*

*Shades of white: ceramics, plastic,
glass and wood*

*Brightly coloured soft plastic
containers and green glass jar*

*Glass and ceramics in
shades of blue*

*Handmade coloured glass vases, wood
cubes, painted ceramics*

*Glass cubes in
soft pastels*

*Black and white in
various shapes*

*Painted wooden cubes, decorated with
ribbon and buttons, and pink ceramic vase*

*Blue Chinese take-away boxes,
and stripes on wood*

Small cool drink bottles can often come in handy as flower pots. Simply use a number together to form a large arrangement. Quarter fill the bottles with water. Cut the flowers to the required length and place in the bottles. Here I have used a variety of flowers, including 'Casa Blanca' lilies, germinis, hypericum berries and Inca lilies in white, dark pink, and apricot. This kind of arrangement serves well as a table decoration or as a striking statement in a kitchen window.

Planning

When you plan an arrangement for a particular space, you need to take a number of factors into account.

Will the arrangement be on show during the day or at night? Is the light adequate?

Lighting plays an equally important role as colour in the atmosphere that is created by the arrangement. If the arrangement is to stand where the light is dim, the use of white, light yellow or light pink flowers with darker foliage would be the best choice. Dark flowers such as red and purple look good during the day, but tend to disappear if the lighting is not good. Even if the arrangement is intended for daytime display and the lighting is poor, the wrong use of colour will make it even less effective.

Although it is not always possible, try to make your arrangement for special occasions at the same time of day for which it is intended. At least view it in the same light that it will enjoy on the occasion (for example, candlelight for a table decoration). In this way you can ensure that you create the perfect atmosphere.

Ensure that the arrangement won't be an irritation, yet at the same time is visible and makes a strong impact. Do not use too many kinds of plant material or colours. A gaudy bunch tends to lose all impact.

Handling & care

When you arrange a bunch of flowers, the idea is not only that it should look attractive, but that it should look attractive for as long as possible. You should therefore choose plant material of the best quality, prepare it properly and take good care of it.

Preparation
This step is usually the one you would like to skip, but only a few minutes will ensure that the flowers last longer and that your arrangement looks attractive for longer.

Picking flowers
If you are privileged to be able to pick flowers and greenery out of your own garden, do so in the early morning or late afternoon when it is not too hot and the rate of evaporation of moisture from the plant is not too fast. Carry a bucket of water with you and immediately place the cut flowers in it. It is also good to avoid new growth points, as they wither quickly. Choose unblemished flowers. It is always better to pick flowers that are not fully open.

Snip the stems
If you are not able to place the cut flowers in water immediately, it is advisable to cut about 2 cm from the stems before you place them in water. Also do this if you have bought or been given a bunch of flowers which was out of water for some time.

Cut the flower stems at an angle to increase the surface that will absorb water. Place snipped flower stems in water immediately to avoid their exposure to air. Always use sharp scissors or a sharp knife so that you do not bruise the stem. Flowers with thick stems such as sunflowers and dahlias should also be cut at an angle or even vertically to increase water absorption.

Seal the stems
Plants with milky stems such as poppies should be burnt with a flame or doused in boiling water to seal the point of the stem. This slows the rate of water absorption and prevents the stems from drawing in air and then wilting.

Woody stems
Most greenery and some flowers have woody stems that draw water up with difficulty. Scrape the last 5 cm of bark-like fibre from the outside of the stem with a knife. After that, cut the stems at an angle. Water absorption can also be improved by cutting the stems vertically up the middle or bruising them with a hammer. These stems must then be placed in deep water so that they absorb maximum amounts of water and thus ensure a longer lifespan in the arrangement. Greenery with woody stems can also be placed wholly under the water for a couple of hours. Some roses also have woody stems. When you buy or pick roses it is always advisable to remove the thorns, not only so that they do not prick you, but also to ensure that it is not difficult to arrange them. They can be cut off one by one with scissors or a knife, or you can use a rose stripper.

When your flowers have wilted
Boiling water can be used to give new life to flowers such as tulips, sunflowers and Barberton daisies (Gerberas). Stand the flowers in boiling water until they start to pick up. The use of boiling water lengthens the lifespan of flowers by ridding the stems

of air bubbles and bacteria. Make use of a container with a narrow spout or a cloth to ensure that the flower heads are not damaged by steam. Wilted flowers can sometimes be resuscitated by holding the entire flower stem under water for a few minutes and then cutting the bottom of the stem. You must be careful though to shake all the water from the flower head to prevent it from rotting.

When to pick

Many flowers, especially peonies, roses, irises and poppies, last longer if they are picked when the buds are just ripe, in other words when the colour begins to show. Flowers such as gladioli and delphiniums are ripe for picking when some of the buds are open and the rest are just about to. You can pick open flowers but remember that they will soon wilt. Some garden flowers do not last long in a vase. Keep them for a special occasion when they have to look good for only one day.

Ask how old they are

When you buy flowers, don't be shy to ask the florist how old they are and how long you can expect them to last. Most cut flowers last for five days. The more delicate varieties and those that have a perfume do not generally last as long. Cultivated flowers are specially treated after harvesting to ensure that they last longer than garden flowers.

Clean up

Remove the leaves and small twigs that will be under the water. These leaves could cause rot that will make the water milky and also give off a most unpleasant smell. This will also cause the rest of the flower stem to wilt sooner. Chrysanths are particularly

sensitive in this respect. Clean these stems by holding them firmly in one hand and using the other hand to strip the leaves downwards. For flowers with large blooms it is easier to break or cut them off one by one.

Flower stems made up of different flower buds, such as gladioli and tuberoses (*Polianthes tuberosa*), have buds at the top that in all likelihood will not open. Remove them so that the buds lower down can make better use of the water supply and last longer. Wilted lower buds can be removed for the same reason.

Hollow stems

Flowers such as delphiniums have hollow stems. To ensure that water gets to the flower head as soon as possible, hold it upside down and pour water into it. When the stem is full of water, you can plug it with wet cotton wool or you can put it in water (preferably in the pot in which you are to arrange it) while you keep the hollow closed with the tip of your finger.

Environment

Do not place a bunch of flowers in direct sharp sunlight. Avoid a draught when you display an arrangement. The wind causes faster evaporation and the flowers then draw up more water. The result is that they then wilt faster.

Ensure a long life

Remove wilted buds and change the water regularly. You can add plant food or a teaspoon of sugar and bleach to the water to lengthen the lifespan of your flowers.

It is relatively easy to care for a bunch of flowers if you follow these steps.

Colour

Owing to the fact that colour has an enormous impact on our senses, colour combination is very important in the arrangement of flowers. It plays a determining role in the atmosphere that you create.

• Red speaks of passion, love and energy.

• Blue is soft on the eye and creates a calm atmosphere.
• Yellow shines with warm friendship.
• Orange is proud, flamboyant and young.
• Purple is regal.
• Green is fresh, but also creates a peaceful feeling.
• White is light and is symbolic of purity.

Combinations

With the use of warm colours such as red, orange and yellow together you can create a striking bright arrangement. Yellow and white flowers are ideal for brightening a dark space. Shades of yellow with purple, green and blue (their complementary colours on the colour wheel) will create an equally strong impact.

Colours such as green, blue and purple, which adjoin one another on the colour wheel, create a harmonious colour scheme. The use of complementary colours (those that are opposite one another on the colour wheel) ensure striking and bright arrangements. Cooler colours such as a bluey pink, light purple, blue and purple create a delicate and calming effect. Grey foliage such as bluegum twigs (*Eucalyptus cineria*) complemens these colous perfectly.

Monochromatic arrangements consist of flowers of only one colour. A quiet, peaceful effect is created by using shades of the same colour, such as in this example, where dark blue and light blue delphiniums are arranged in a pot with blue patterns.

Delphiniums have hollow stems, so snip them under the water to ensure that no air bubbles are drawn up causing the flowers to wilt.

When bright yellow (the complementary colour) is used in the same arrangement, it creates a completely different effect and brightens the arrangement. None of these arrangements are more correct than the others; it comes down to personal taste and what is suitable for the specific occasion or surrounding, and the purpose for which it is intended and the atmosphere you wish to create.

The colour of your arrangement can be complemented by the background against which you place it. Light flowers stand out against a dark background and in the same way dark flowers stand out against a light background. You should also carefully choose the colour of the foliage that you will use in the arrangement to ensure that the flowers do not disappear.

In the photographs above the same bunch of lavender is displayed in different coloured containers.

Note the distinct effect of harmonious (blue, green pots), complementary (orange pot) and neutral (cream pot) colours.

The photograph below demonstrates the successful foil of a blue wall to show off the white containers and reddish flowers to best effect.

Flowers & foliage

The the main flowers and foliage species used for the arrangements featured in the book have been listed and illustrated here. They are all easy to find at most flower shops, and many will grow in gardens all over the country. If you cannot find a specific type of flower, substitute it with a flower of similar shape and colour.

Alstroemeria (Inca lily)

Anemone coronaria (Anemone)

Antirrhinum majus (Snapdragon)

Asparagus densiflorus
(Foxtail)

Aspidistra elatior
(Aspidistra)

Aster novi-belgii
(Michealmas daisy)

Banksia hookerana

Berzelia lanuginosa
(Kolkol)

Brassica oleracea
(Ornamental kale)

Camellia japonica
(Camellia)

Centaurea cyanus
(Corn flower)

Chondropetalum (Eligia tectorum) (Reed)

Chrysanthemum x hybrida (Chrysanths)

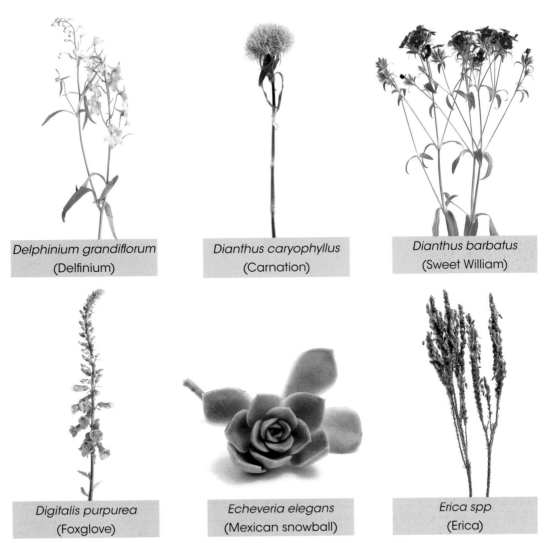

Delphinium grandiflorum
(Delfinium)

Dianthus caryophyllus
(Carnation)

Dianthus barbatus
(Sweet William)

Digitalis purpurea
(Foxglove)

Echeveria elegans
(Mexican snowball)

Erica spp
(Erica)

Eryngium maritimum
(Sea holly)

Eucalyptus cinerea
(Eucalyptus)

Eustoma grandiflorum
(Lisianthus)

Freesia
(Freesia)

Gerbera
(Barberton daisy)

Gladiolus
(Gladiolus)

Hedera
(Ivy)

Hypericum x inodorum
(Hypericum)

Iris (Iris)

Kalanchoe

Lathyrus odoratus (Sweet peas)

Lavandula (Lavender)

Leucospermum cordifolium
(Pincussion)

Lilium
(Lily)

Lilium "Stargazer"
("Stargazer" lily)

Matthiola incana
(Stocks)

Mimetes hottentoticus
(Mimetes)

Molucella laevis
(Irish bells)

Paeonia (Pionies)

Papaver (Poppies)

Protea grandiceps (Protea)

Protea cynaroides x madiba (King protea)

Rosa spp. (Rose)

Sedum

Tulipa
(Tulip)

Zantedeschia aethiopica
(Arum lily)

Instant arrangements

Most of us live such busy lives these days that we do not have much time to spend on flower arranging. But we would still like to give a special identity to our homes and personal spaces. Fortunately help is available in the form of interesting containers and it is actually easy, using single blooms, to create something striking in the blink of an eye. What follows are a few relatively simple ideas for instant arrangements.

Long-lasting pleasure

Buy yourself an orchid
(*Phalaenopsis amabis* 'White')
and plant it in a special
orchid growing medium in
an interesting pot with holes
under it. Choose a plant with
lots of buds and few flowers.
In this way you will ensure
an extended flowering time.
Do a little research on the
maintenance of this special
plant; a subject all on its own.

Keep Phalaenopsis varieties'
roots moist in a well drained
medium. Place in areas with
a moderate temperature
(20 – 30 °C) and high humidity.
They grow in trees in the wild, so
avoid direct sunlight.

Water twice a week and allow
the water to drain completely.

Short and tall

Place just a few flowers in interesting containers. The tumbling dark red of this amaranthus (*Amaranthus caudatus*) complements the fine red pin heads in the pincushion protea (*Leucospermum cordifolium*).

The orangey pink of the pincushions and the deep red of the amaranthus also contrast with the blue wall. Although the pots and the flowers form interesting shapes, as a whole the arrangement makes a minimalist picture.

Lilies and boughs
Dané Erwee

Dané Erwee of Okasie created this unusual arrangement. Press small straight boughs vertically into a holder containing oasis. Then arrange the lilies in between the boughs. The contrast between the rough boughs and the strong but delicate lilies forms a striking picture, ideal for an entrance hall or on a large table.

Tip

Remove the pollen heads. They not only discolour the leaves, but also anything else with which they come in contact. If they have already stained something, wind adhesive tape around your finger with the sticky side outside, and carefully lift the pollen from the material. Do not try to brush it off, as this will only make the stain worse.

Feathered Barberton daisies

Here I have arranged variously coloured Barberton daisies (*Gerbera*) in different coloured plastic containers with coloured feathers fastened with wire. It creates the illusion that the feathers are floating freely in the air around the arrangement. This kind of arrangement is a clever table decoration for a young girl's birthday or bedroom. The choice of shades is endless. You can use any brightly coloured flowers for such an arrangement.

Iris simplicity

Two or three bunches of irises in a
simple glass vase need nothing
further to show them to advantage.
When you arrange flowers in a
vase, the stems tend to move each
time you place a new flower in the
arrangement. It is generally much
easier to arrange the flowers in your
hand, to clip the stems, and place the
flowers just so in the container. Then
you can adjust the flowers here and
there as necessary.

Tip
Soil often clings between the stems
and leaves of flowers such as irises
and tulips. Ensure that you remove the
leaves and rinse off the soil especially
if you are using a glass container.

Camellia stem

The loveliest blooms often come out of your own garden or a friend's! This camellia (*Camellia japonica*) came from Dané's garden and I was able to play beautifully with its arrangement. Note how entirely different it looks placed in different containers.

Fill a container with gel crystals and place the small branch with its stem on this base. To ensure that the arrangement is fully appreciated, place it on a low coffee table.

Alternatively place it in a container with a narrow mouth or use glass beads to balance the arrangement in a container with a wider mouth. For something different, thread a few beads on florist's wire and allow them to glide in the air and in this way form part of the arrangement.

 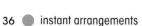

Purple partners

You can make an arrangement using more than one container. Here I have used two identical pots in which I have placed different flowers of the same colour. I have formed separate bunches of purple anemones and lavender and placed them in the pots. The upright lavender stems balance the open, flat ranunculus calyxes.

Threefold enjoyment

Peonies are very special flowers and sometimes it is necessary to make the simplest of arrangements so that their beauty can be fully appreciated. Place single blooms in glass vases and stand them in front of a mirror so that you can enjoy them from every angle.

Striking contrast

This combination of green carnations (*Dianthus*) and miniature roses is strikingly lovely. Line the silver container with black plastic before you place the prepared oasis, so that the latter is not visible.
Snip the plastic just below the rim of the container, so that it is also not visible once the arrangement has been completed. Form a base of the green carnations and place the roses evenly in the arrangement and slightly higher than the carnations. If the rose buds are still slightly closed, allow enough space so that when they open they will not look crowded. The complementary red and green colours work beautifully together. This kind of low arrangement is ideal for table settings as it will not impede the sociability around the table.

Roses and rust

These rust-coloured containers complement the colour and the form of the roses in
a special manner. Arrange the roses in your
hand and then place them carefully in the
cups, or tie them first with raffia.

These mini arrangements form perfect gifts
for each place setting when you invite your
friends for a special tea. You can also use
old china teacups, milk jugs and teapots
filled with flowers. Place them in the centre
of the table as a table decoration.

Fun with peonies

Peonies are striking flowers. Arrange them very simply and without additional greenery. Distribute the varied colours evenly through the arrangement. (Opposite)

A fish bowl makes an ideal container for flowers such as peonies. It has a nice narrow mouth and a plump base of transparent glass through which the green stems can be seen. First create a bunch in your hand and then place it carefully in the container.

Place the peonies evenly in a simple wooden container. This container holds a glass vase inside, which is filled with glass marbles to hold the peonies in position.

Bundle cellophane loosely inside the container so that it forms an oasis that will hold the flowers in position. Now place the peonies one by one in the vase.

Poppies and glass

The simplicity of poppies in a glass
container will brighten any corner of your
home. Seal the stems with boiling water
to help the blooms last longer. The easiest
way in which to arrange them is to hold
them upside down and pack their stems
tightly together. All the stems must lie in
the same direction, as if you were making
a posy. Then turn the whole arrangement
upright and place it in the container.

Poppy four-play

These four glass containers are filled with
gel crystals. The poppy stems are cut into
different lengths and then placed. Burn
the stems briefly to ensure that the leaves
do not drop too soon. This delays water
absorption which will enable the flowers to
open more quickly, but at the same time it
prevents the absorption of air bubbles that
causes wilting.

The family silverware

Antique silverware is in itself striking, but with the addition of a single lovely bloom it becomes more eye-catching. If the silverware is no longer watertight, or you are afraid of damaging it, you can place another container inside it. If you are using air plants, it is obviously not necessary to add water. Small arrangements such as these are not only are impressive in a collective display, they can also be used individually or grouped as table decorations.

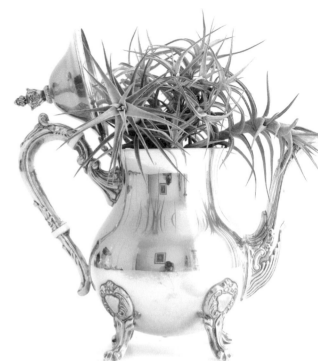

Tillandsia (air plant)

Anemone (anemones)

Dianthus barbatus (sweet Williams)

Dianthus (carnations)

Chrysanthemum (large white chrysanthemums)

Lathyrus odoratus (sweet peas)

Leucospermum cordifolium (pincushions)

Freesias in flasks

Fill interesting glass containers
or flasks with a few freesia
blooms (*Freesia*). Place
them bloom by bloom,
or arrange them in
your hand as a bunch,
snipping the stems evenly
before placing them in the
container. If you form the bunch
in your hand, it is important not to
place them so closely together that
they will look crowded. Use the natural
curves of the flower stems to dictate
the shape of the arrangement.

Fragrant gift

A bunch of flowers in a vase that can be displayed immediately makes an easy and welcome gift. The container that I have used here is made of light blue plastic. I first arranged the sweet-smelling white narcissi (*Narcissus spp.*) in a bunch, snipped the stems, and then placed them in the container. Bright blue Petersham ribbon tied around the container completes the arrangement.

Cornflowers in bell jars

Make simple table decorations
by placing single bright
blooms, in this case cornflowers
(*Centauria cyanus*), under bell
jars. If the bloom is not placed
in water, make the arrangement
just before your guests arrive.
You could also fill small flat glass
containers with gel crystals; then
place the flower stalks on them.

Nest of roses

I have used a simple narrow glass mixing bowl here. Fill the container with water and form a rough oasis of dodder to hold the flowers in place.

The 15 rose stems have been cut quite short and positioned in the dodder on the container. Don't crowd the roses, but leave sufficient space for them to open.

Askance display

The striking colour of the pincushion and the container requires nothing more to draw the eye. Pincushions last long enough without water to play their role as table decorations and can be placed in water immediately after the dinner party.

Yesteryear with moss

This pewter container was filled with moss before the two pincushions were placed in it, thus enhancing the 'olde worlde' feeling created by the pewter. Moss that is kept moist makes an outstanding medium for arrangements with an earthy feel.

Easy arrangements

The arrangements in this section require a little more time and knowledge of basic techniques, but but there are clear step by step instructions, often with additional ideas for alternative finishes. Apply these ideas by making use of material and containers available to you, and in this way, place your own stamp on your arrangements.

Proteas in glass

Containers will often determine the nature of your arrangement. As a starting point, bear in mind that you should not confine yourself to simply one idea. This container, for example, can be used as described below, or it could be changed by filling it with coloured water to create an interesting effect, in this way also making use of the hollow of the inner glass.

You will need
glass container
plastic beads
fine willowy twigs
3 proteas
(*Protea grandiceps*)
3 of 4 stems of red chrysanthemums

Fill the space under the container with fine twigs on which beads have been threaded and in which they are roughly bundled. Place a piece of paper under the container so that when you move the arrangement you can prevent the twigs from springing out. When you have completed the arrangement, simply slide the container on the paper. Remove the paper as soon as you are satisfied with the position of the arrangement. Place three proteas in the container. The arrangement can now be finished off with an edge of dark red chrysanthemums, which should be placed around the proteas (make sure that there is enough water in the container to hold the stems of the chrysanthemums). Alternatively you could attach beads to the ends of the twigs with ins and place them in the middle of the proteas. Another option is to thread beads on fine curly twigs and stand them in the middle of the arrangement.

In addition to the colour and form of this indigenous flower, I also like the contrast between delicate glass and the large strong protea bloom. The beads were chosen so that their colour complements that of the proteas.

Stylish fynbos

Fynbos is almost the last flower that one would expect to see in this container that resembles a stylish hatbox, but the combination works well. Be adventurous when you combine plants and containers, and surprise yourself.

You will need
container
3 proteas (*Protea grandiceps*)
3 stems *Mimetes spp.*
5 stems kolkol (*Berzelia lanuginosa*)

Fill the container with water and place the three proteas so that only their heads stick out. Now add the Mimetes. Fill the gaps with the cones. This arrangement should last quite some time, as all fynbos are hardwood species. The arrangement is also reasonably low and can be used as a table decoration, but works just as well to brighten a corner in your home.

Tips
If you prefer, you could use oasis. The container for the arrangement will determine if it is necessary.

If you cut the protea stems shorter, keep the off cuts and use them to create structure in other arrangements.

Roses under glass

Red roses are always romantic. This kind of arrangement is ideal for a table decoration for a romantic dinner, as it is not too high. The bell jar and candles allow for the loveliest reflections.

You will need
container
bell jar
10 red roses
Pellaea

Snip the roses to an even length and place them in water. The light blue pot emphasises the red of the roses.

Finish the arrangement off by using fine twigs of pilea. To provide a variation on an ordinary pot for the roses, place a bell jar over the arrangement.

Tips
Cut the rose stems at an angle to ensure that they keep.

It is often easiest to arrange the flowers in your hand and then to place them in the container.

Succulent variety

Sometimes we forget that pot plants can also serve as arrangements. A little bit of green can give life to any room and is especially useful if you do not have a garden. Coarse containers with something earthy are eminently suitable for succulents such as these.

You will need
container
a variety of succulents (*Kalanchoe, Echeveria, Sedum*)
gravel
potting soil

Fill the container with gravel and then with the potting soil. Plant the succulents in the container in a pleasing combination. Succulents do not require much water in order to survive, so although you should water regularly, add only small amounts at a time.

Tip
You can cultivate a new plant by breaking off a small leaf and placing it in wet newspaper until it roots. Succulents grow so easily that you could even stick the leaf straight into the ground.

Tulip fantasy

Tulips are fabulous flowers. They appear quite hard and masculine while still in bud. But after they have been arranged, they grow in all directions, and after they open, they appear soft, feminine and almost fragile. They drink a lot of water in comparison with other flowers. Ensure on a daily basis that there is enough water in the container.

You will need
glass container
10 tulips (*Tulipa*) in the colour of your
   choice

I specifically made use of a glass container so that the striking green stems are not lost. Here I have arranged all the blooms in one direction, but you could also stand them upright in the container. They do not remain exactly as you have arranged them, as you see in this photograph, which was taken a day after the flowers were arranged. Tulips are not static but 'grow' in various directions as they take in water in an arrangement such as this.

Tips

When you buy tulips, their stems are often brown where they have been cut. Cut about 2 cm off the stems.

If there is soil between the leaves and the stem, rinse well, especially if you are using a glass container for the arrangement. Remove any spoilt leaves and those that will be covered with water.

Take-away ranuculus

A take-away container works exceptionally well for a gift arrangement. It is advisable to use a deep container so that transporting the gift is easier.

You will need
Chinese take-away plastic container
container for flowers and water
dodder
2 bunches of ranunculus (*Ranunculus asiaticus*)

Fill the container with water. Create a supporting framework out of the dodder. Do not pack the dodder too thickly in the container, as this can interfere with the arranging process (especially as ranunculus have soft stems). Arrange the ranunculus so that their colours are evenly spread. Begin at the edges and work towards the middle. Finish the arrangement off with more dodder.

A bunch of flowers in a jug

Alwyn Burger

A water or milk jug makes a pretty container for a bunch of flowers or herbs out of your garden.

You will need
container
mixed flowers (bought or freshly picked)
raffia

In this bunch Alwyn used ornamental kale (*Brassica oleracea*), 'Stargazer' lilies, yellow irises, fynbos, lavender, ranunculus, anemones, sweet williams, a 'Black baccara' rose, a red rose, green dianthus, kolkol (*Berzelia lanuginosa*) and *Banksia*. Arrange the flowers in your hand so that their colours and shapes complement one another and the bunch has a pleasing form. Tie the bunch firmly with raffia without bruising the plant material.

Then place it in the container with enough water. This kind of arrangement can brighten up your kitchen, but is also suitable to beautify an outdoor table that has been laid for a meal.

Tip
Make a bunch of flowers that you have tied together if you do not wish to use oasis. In this way the flowers will stay in the water just as you have placed them, while otherwise they may move around.

Elegant minimalism

Sometimes you need little more than a single arum lily and a special glass vase to create something truly unique. This arrangement by Alwyn Burger of Okasie demonstrates what one can achieve with a minimum of material.

You will need
tall glass container
dry branch that fits
6 arum lilies (*Zantedeschia aethiopica*)
florist's wire

Choose a branch that fits the container of your choice. Immerse it for a few minutes in boiling water to destroy most of the micro-organisms on the surface. Place the branch in a container filled with water to which you have added a little bleach. This will inhibit further growth of micro-organisms.

Arrange the arums in the container as shown in the photo. The stems are flexible and two of the flowers have been hooked around the container and tied together with florist's wire and for an unusual finish.

The combination of boiling water and bleach reduce micro-organism and keep the water clear. Some kinds of dry wood will eventually cause dicolouration of the water but the bleach should prevent this too.

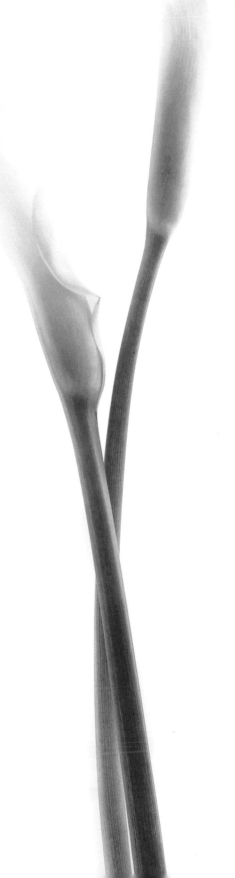

Fantastic in plastic

These days really clever plastic-bag containers are available in a variety of colours and sizes. These are perfect to create fun arrangements in an instant. Here a single flower works perfectly in combination with a second completely submerged in a clear container.

You will need
plastic-bag container
florist's wire (medium thickness)
Barberton daisies (*Gerbera*)

Pour water into the plastic container to open and anchor it. Stabelise one of the flowers with florist's wire: Thread the wire through the bottom of one of the flowers. Bend the tip of the wire and pull it gently back so that it hooks into the flower centre. Wind the remaining wire carefully around the flower stem (see page 85). This will help to keep the flower upright. Place in position in the container. Cut the stem of another bloom very short and place it in the container submerged at the foot of the wired flower.

Tips
Gerbera prefers a low level of water. Ensure that you regularly add fresh water.
When you make a table arrangement, take the height of the arrangement and its density into account, so that guests will be able to see through it. The best way to check if an arrangement is likely to bother your guests is to place it on the table and judge it yourself from a seated position.

Tulip embrace

Choosing the right flowers for interesting containers such as this, is often quite a challenge. In this case we used tulips to suit the clean lines of the pot. Arums (*Zantedeschia aethiopica*) will also work well in this container.

You will need
container (this one is from Okasie)
1 bunch tulips (*Tulipa*)
fine florist's wire

Ensure that the container is filled to the top with water, not only for the well-being of the flowers, but also to give the arrangement weight. Remove any torn leaves, rinse any soil off, and place the flowers in the container one by one so that the longest stems are closest to the fork in the pot. Bind the stems of these two blooms together with fine wire or fishing line so that they balance one another and form a curve towards the centre of the arrangement.

For the sake of the vase

What a striking vase! If you are concerned that your arrangement will detract from a unique container, keep it simple. The colour in the vase is repeated in the choice of yellow chrysanthemums and orange Gerbera. In addition I also chose green carnations and a simple broad green leaf.

You will need

container

3 stems yellow chrysanthemums
(*Chrysanthemum*)

1 orange Barberton daisy (*Gerbera*)

5 stems green carnations (*Dianthus*)

broad green leaf

florist's wire

raffia

dodder

Thread florist's wire through the leaf so that you can manipulate its shape as desired. Work carefully to avoid bruising and discolouring the leaf. To make the arrangement step by step, simply place the flowers in the container one at a time in the order in which they are listed.

As a more formal alternative, Alwyn Burger of Okasie used the same flowers in a bunch. The leaf is folded over and bound together with the same flowers. The arrangement is finished off with single stems of dodder.

Bunches

It is so easy to walk into a florist's shop and choose a bunch of flowers in the wink of an eye. But it is easier than you think to create your own equally professional bunch. Choose long stems of foliage that will give height. Sword fern works well for this purpose. Add a flower of the same length. Then add flowers such as roses, proteas and lilies that will form focal points. The flowers that you use as fillers will depend on your own personal taste, the occasion, the space in which they are to be placed, and the container. Small flowers such as Michaelmas daisies and baby's breath (*Gypsophila*) provide a wispy appearance, while chrysanths provide more structure.

You will need

1 bunch cream and 1 bunch rust coloured chrysanths (*Chrysanthemum*)
1 bunch foxgloves (*Digitalis purpurea*)
5 pincushions
3 large white chrysanths (*Chrysanthemum*)
raffia
2 sheets tissue paper

Clean the last two-thirds of the stems. Begin to make your arrangement by placing two flower stems across one another. Add a third stem to cross with these two.

Turn the arrangement slightly in your hand and add a few more stems. Ensure that all the stems cross over in the same direction. The stems will soon form a spiral. Distribute the flowers evenly from the outset. Try to arrange the same flowers at the same level. It will help if you keep a mirror nearby, especially if you are making a large bunch, so that you ensure a balanced arrangement while you are in the process of making it. If you are using only a few large blooms (such as the large white chrysanths in this example), leave them till last. You can place them afterwards. Simply ensure that you place the stems in the same direction as the rest of the bunch. In this way you will achieve a more even spread of the large blooms. Bind the bunch tightly with raffia and snip the stems to an even length.

A good test of balance is if the bunch stands upright after it has been bound.

To finish off the arrangement, fold two squares of tissue paper diagonally. Hold the bunch upside down and place the middle of the folded side where the flowers have been bound. Do the same with the second sheet of paper. You could use adhesive tape to glue the sheets together, but if you work correctly all you need is another piece of raffia or a piece of ribbon to tie the paper. And voila! There you have a lovely wrapped gift. You could also use brown paper or plastic instead of tissue paper. A length of lace will also make a lovely alternative to ribbon or raffia.

The last photo demonstrates how you can place exactly the same bunch in a container – it's just as lovely!

Another bunch

Use this arrangement as an example and choose plant material of your choice. You could also use plant material from your own garden. If you are not sure that the flowers or foliage from your garden are suitable for arranging, snip off a small stem and place it in water to see how it lasts. You will soon see if it works or not.

You will need
plant material of your choice
or
a bought or given bouquet
container(s)
raffia

When you wish to arrange mixed flowers for a vase, it is easiest to make them into a bunch and then to place them. You can always place the flowers in the vase one by one, but this doesn't necessarily make for a neat arrangement, especially if you are using a glass container and the stems move around each time you place the next one. Otherwise, after you have arranged the bunch, cut the stems to the right length and place the arrangement in the vase.

Sometimes you may discover that you have misjudged the size of the container. If it is too small, you cannot simply strangle the flowers and force them in. And if the mouth of your vase is too large, all the flowers fall to the outside and you are stuck with a 'bald patch' in the middle! If your vase is of such a nature that it will disguise the raffia, you can tie the bunch with raffia and place it in the vase bound. Alternatively it would be advisable to simply add more flowers.

A bunch of flowers can easily look cheap and sparse if it is not generous and full.

When you receive a bunch of flowers as a gift, remove the paper, snip the stems to the desired length, and place in a pot with water, as is. Neaten the bunch slightly, but do your best to keep the original shape. If the bunch came with flower food, add it to the water.

A formal outdoors arrangement

Sometimes one would like to make an arrangement for use outdoors, for instance when entertaining on the patio. Use a container such as a rusted urn that suits the outdoor setting. It will look good, is heavy and will not easily fall over or break. It will not be watertight, so line it with cellophane and then position the oasis. A plastic bag will work just as well. It is important though to cut the bag below the mouth of the container and make sure that it does not show when the arrangement is finished. Use dodder to help disguise the plastic.

Tip
Remove the topmost buds from the gladioli to ensure that the remaining buds all open. This will ensure that the arrangement stays good for longer.

You will need
iron pot
prepared oasis
cellophane or plastic bag
dodder
1 bunch gladioli (*Gladiolus*)
2 bunches foxtail (*Asparagus densiflorus*)

Line the container with cellophane or plastic to make it watertight. Place all ten gladioli vertically in the centre of the arrangement. Plants such as gladioli can easily damage the oasis as the stems are thick, causing your whole arrangement to fall apart. You should thus ensure that you do not force too many stems into a small area. The rest of the oasis is filled with the foxtail, which is a useful plant to keep in your garden for instant greenery.

Chinks in a fishbowl

Have you ever wondered what to do with that old fishbowl? Use flowers with flexible stems such as Chincherinchee (pig's ears or tulips would also work), and make use of the transparent glass to create something unusual. And if you do not have an old fishbowl, acquire one or two in different sizes. This kind of arrangement often looks more complicated than it really is and does not use a lot of flowers.

You will need
2 round glass bowls of different sizes
2 bunches Chincherinchee (*Ornithogalum*)
1 bunch Barberton daisies (*Gerbera*)
florist's wire (medium)

Fill the bowl with water and arrange the chincherinchees in a spiral. Make sure that the ends of the stems stems are in the water. Do the same with the smaller container. Thread the wire through the bottom of the gerbera. Bend the tip of the wire and pull it gently back so that it hooks into the flower centre. Wind the remaining wire carefully around the flower stem Rest gerberas lightly between the chinks.

Arrangements in glass make the best display if they are placed where light is reflected from both the glass and the water.

Lilies in dodder

This is an excellent way of using lilies together with coarse greenery that preferably does not itself get wet. With the help of plastic water tubes the arrangement remains largely dry and you do not need to make the container watertight. Unfortunately the flowers must be removed one by one for the water to be replenished, so do buy the biggest tubes you can find so that this does not have to be done too often. While you're at it, snip the stems of the flowers to improve water absorption.

water source, in the ball of dodder. This is a simple and relatively inexpensive way to create a large arrangement. Lilies do not like wind, so only place the arrangement outside if you know that wind won't be a problem. You also don't necessarily need to use lilies for the arrangement.

Wired Barberton daisies, roses and tulips will work just as well. But you must remember that some flowers are very thirsty and that you will have to fill the small tubes with water regularly.

You will need

large container
dodder
10 stems "Stargazer" lilies
plastic water tubes (available at florist shops)

Form a ball of dodder and place it in the container. Cut the tips of the lily stems, fill the small tubes with water, and place a lily in each. Arrange the lilies, each in its own

Tip

Remove the pollen heads. They not only discolour the leaves, but also anything else with which they come in contact. If they have already stained something, wind adhesive tape around your finger with the sticky side outside, and carefully lift the pollen from the material. Do not try to brush it off, as this will only make the stain worse.

Roses in a bucket

Create a simple but striking table arrangement with just one bunch of roses in a bucket. Do not use a tall container that will irritate the guests around the table.

You will need
1 bunch (20) roses
container
oasis

Place the prepared oasis in the container and add a small amount of water. Cut the roses to the desired length and use the foliage, as shown in the photo, as greenery.

Make your cut just above a bud from which another leaf or stem would shoot. This will form a finer point and make it easier to arrange in the oasis. It will also assist in the drawing up of water. Now arrange the roses in the container. As I have used a galvanised iron bucket, I have not arranged the roses formally and I have left them at different lengths in order to form layers. I have complemented the arrangement on the table with miniature buckets, each with one rose bloom and a leaf in it. Try using one of these small buckets at each place setting for a different effect.

Roses in tulip bowls

You can put this kind of arrangement together in the container, or make it first in your hand, then place it in the container and finally add the finishing touches. This container with its wide mouth can hold a large bouquet of flowers.

You will need
1 bunch (20) roses
1 bunch baby's breath (*Gypsophila paniculata*)
flower pot

Fill the container of your choice with water and arrange the baby's breath. Gypsophila is the ideal filler for a container with a wide mouth, as it consists of bunches of fine stems which help to hold the roses in place. Clean the stems of the roses, but retain the last two leaf stems to give fullness to the bunch. You could strip the stems completely and use other greenery if you prefer, but the natural greenery provided by the rose leaves complements the roses. Place the roses evenly in the pot. Be careful not to break the gypsophila stems or to place the flowers too closely together. Tease the gypsophila out a little when the arrangement is complete.

Lilies and lisianthus

When you buy lilies and lisianthus for an arrangement, it is wise to choose blooms that are still closed. The buds of these two flowers open nicely in a container. Lilies can last up to three or four weeks in a container (but be sure to follow the tips below). This container with its rich jewel-like colours shows the flowers off beautifully.

You will need
container
1 bunch (10 stems) "Stargazer" lilies
1 bunch (10 stems) violet coloured
   lisianthus (*Eustoma grandiflorum*)

Three-quarter fill the container of your choice with water. Remove the leaves that will be under the water and those that are damaged. Make the arrangement in your hand as described before so that the stems form a spiral. Snip at least 2 cm from the stems in a straight line to compensate for the time they were out of the water while you were arranging them. Now place the arrangement in the water and adjust it as required.

Tips
If you want the flowers to last as long as possible, do not place them in a draught. Lilies in particular do not like wind. The reason for this is simple: the wind causes moisture to evaporate quickly through the leaves, which then speeds up the osmosis of water, resulting in the flowers opening fully and then quickly wilt.

Change the water often and use plant food. This will keep the water clean and will serve as a source of nourishment.

In a leaf on a mirror

For this kind of arrangement you can place the flowers in any pattern on the leaf. As a flat arrangement it is ideal for a table decoration. Its severe lines also make it an ideal decoration for a men's function. The mirror box ensures lovely reflections when candles are placed in square glass holders on the table. To create an entirely different ambience, place the arrangement in a wooden box.

You will need
container with reflective (mirror) sides
oasis
leaf of a giant strelitzia or wild banana
  (*Strelitzia nicolai*)
poppy seed heads (*Papaver*)
chrysanths (*Chrysanthemum*)
Craspedia heads

First measure the oasis to make sure that it will fit easily into the container. Take it out again. Cut the leaf of the giant strelitzia or wild banana so that it will cover the upper surface of the oasis and is slightly longer on one side to fold over. Cut another piece to the same size. Cover the oasis with one piece of leaf. You could attach it to the oasis with a pin or two. Place the other leaf at a right angle over the first. The oasis should now be completely covered. Place the oasis in the container. Make small holes in the leaf before you begin to push the flower stems through. Make the first row diagonal (from side to side). Place the other flowers row by row until the container is filled diagonally across from one side to the other.

Regal simplicity

King proteas remain one of our most beautiful indigenous flowers and need few additions to be shown off to their best advantage. Hessian has been used here around the glass container to hide the stems, so that the giant flower heads remain the focal point.

You will need
container
2 proteas (*Protea cynaroides*)
air plants (*Tillandsia*)
poppy seed heads (*Papaver*)
hessian
raffia

Fill a square glass container with water. Place the proteas in the container and fill the remaining space with the air plants, which naturally do not need to be in the water. They will now serve as a framework for the poppy seed heads. Ensure that the stems of the poppy seed heads do reach the water.

Wrap the hessian around the container and secure it with raffia.

On a grand scale

It was once the fashion (and may still be, in fact) to place large empty pots in a row in the garden. These pots can also come in handy if you want to make arrangements of large flowers.

You will need
large container
plastic bucket or container that fits in
  the pot
proteas (*Protea cynaroides* and
  P. cynaroides x madiba)
dodder
reeds

Fill the pot with newspaper so that it will support the container that you choose. If the container is too small for the pot, newspaper will also ensure that it doesn't fall about inside the pot. Use dodder to disguise the container in the pot. Make a large ball of dodder to serve as a base for the arrangement. Now arrange the proteas close to the side of the container. Roll dodder in balls like balls of wool, and use it as greenery to fill the gaps. Create height by positioning three groups of reeds in one corner of the arrangement.

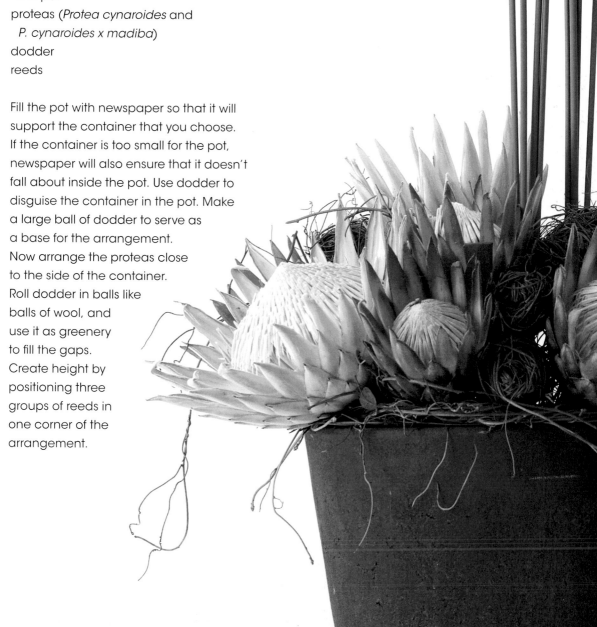

More challenging arrangements

These arrangements present more of a challenge and will take longer to complete. However, it is within everyone's reach to tackle any one of them. The step-by-step instructions will give you confidence in using new techniques. You can apply these techniques to create arrangements in your own style.

Hotchpotch

This pot is absolutely unique. My great-grandmother made it using pieces of broken china from plates and cups, old toy cars and so on, fastened with putty to an old aluminium pot. Dané Erwee of Okasie chose a most unusual combination of plant material to go with it: an aloe, a desert plant if you like; proteas belonging to the fynbos family; and subtropical orchids. The colours are soft but the structure is strong, so that the unique container does not overpower the flowers.

You will need
container
prepared oasis
1 aloe (*Aloe arborenscens*)
2 proteas (*Protea grandiceps*)
8 orchid stems (*Cymbidium spp*)
willow twigs
2 upright stems (in this case protea stems)

Use the oasis to keep the flowers in place. The aloe is used for greenery in this arrangement. Place the aloe in the pot so that it faces forwards.

Fill the container with light yellow orchids that are placed upright in the oasis. Place willow twigs, fastened together, with their leaves between the orchids so that they form a frame over the arrangement. The fine twigs of willow echo the green of the aloe. Place two pink proteas close to the aloe. One protea must be slightly higher than the other to form a slight diagonal line. Finish the arrangement off by placing the two aloe stems on the opposite side. One is again placed deeper than the other.

Olde worlde charm

The typical scent of the bluegum greenery adds to the nostalgia of this olde worlde mixed arrangement.

You will need
container
oasis
1 or 2 bluegum twigs (*Eucalyptus*)
3 to 5 snapdragons (*Antirrhinums*)
3 to 5 yellow kolkol (*Berzelia lanuginosa*)
3 to 5 white chrysanths or asters
   (*Chrysanthemum*)
3 to 5 green carnations (*Dianthus*)
5 roses

Prepare the oasis and place it in the container. Start with the greenery: in this case bluegum stems. The silver grey leaves create a neutral background that will suit any flower colour. Use the natural shape of the branches to guide you. Use the greenery to form a framework, but do not fill the container with too much of the latter.

Also use some of the greenery in the middle of the arrangement. Arrange the snapdragons in two groups immediately opposite one another. The shape of the snapdragons and the bluegum stems require that they are used towards the bottom of the arrangement so that it looks as if they are tumbling from the side of the container. The colour of the snapdragons is now echoed in the yellow fynbos cones. Now do the same with the chrysanths (arranged here in three groups), the green carnation and the roses.

Tip
The flowers can be displayed in a group like this, or as single stems. Flowers arranged in groups have a more structured form, whilst single blooms create a freer appearance. The style will thus depend on the feeling that you would like to create. Depending on the size of the arrangement and the nature of the flowers, you could place one, two, three or even five groups of flowers together.

Natural and organic

This container inspired me to use natural and organic material. It is an ordinary square plastic pot – the kind you use for pot plants. It is decorated with sticks and moss – and hey presto, you have a brand new unique pot (Okasie). You could go for contrast and arrange roses in it, or you could, as I have done here, use indigenous plant material.

You will need
container
prepared oasis
weeping willow stems
dodder
fynbos (*Erica, Chondropetalum,
  Berzelia lanuginosa*)
3 stems Mimetes
plastic netting
florist's wire

Place the oasis in the container. To begin, place willow branches in the corners of the pot. Place dodder around the sides of the pot to disguise it and keep the willow in position. The flower stems should be arranged so that they stand quite upright. Also arrange them in groups in the oasis to provide definition. With bushy flowers such as fynbos types, definition is important. Lastly arrange the Mimetes.

To finish off the arrangement, gently bend the ends of the willow stems and fasten them together with wire to frame it. The colour of the Mimetes is echoed in the brightly coloured plastic orange bag netting tied around the pot. This makes for a cheeky finish by introducing something synthetic into the overall organic feel of the arrangement.

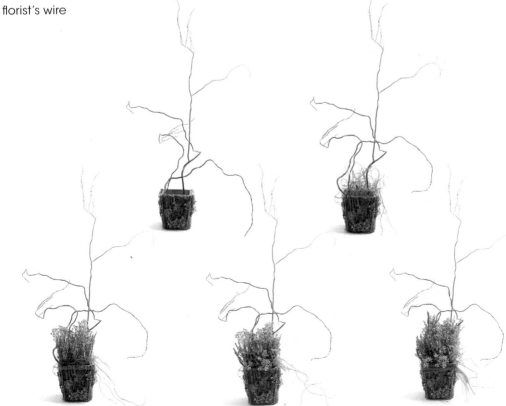

Soft and silver

I wanted to fill this lovely silver container with soft colours, although something bright red would work just as well. If the container is not watertight, line it with cellophane, in which you then place the wet oasis that has been cut to size. Trim the cellophane around the edge of the container so that it will not show when the arrangement is complete.

You will need

container
prepared oasis
several bluegum stems (*Eucalyptus*)
1 bunch lavender (*Lavandula dentata*)
1 bunch light pink roses
1 bunch white roses

Place the oasis in the container and arrange bluegum stems around the edges. Owing to the nature of the holder, all the flowers should be arranged more or less vertically. Small bunches of lavender are then placed in the container, so that they stand out amongst the other flowers. Single stems of lavender will get lost against the coarse bluegum stems. The white and pink roses now fill the remaining space in the container.

Tip

Remember to leave enough space for the roses if they are still in bud when you arrange them. This ensures that the arrangement does not look crowded when they finally open.

Roses in an urn

Throughout the world, roses remain the most popular flower, and although they can be over-used, their delicate beauty remains at the same time decadent, over-the-top, and romantic. Arranged in this Versailles-type urn, they look stunning.

You will need
container
prepared oasis
2 bunches of roses in shades of your choice

Ensure that the oasis is wet and cut to the right size so that it sits firmly in the container. If the pot leaks, line it with a plastic bag or cellophane and then place the oasis. Fill the container to the brim with water. Make a rough estimate of the shape and form of the arrangement and mark the required height with flowers or cut stems. Start by arranging the roses around the edges of the container and work towards the centre. Ensure that the roses are not too close together, so that they have space to open nicely.

Tips

It is sometimes difficult to estimate how long it takes for roses to open, but you will be surprised how quickly this happens after they have been placed in an oasis. Make this arrangement the day before you need it so that the roses have a chance to open.

Do not cut the rose stems too short. You can always adjust the length later, but if you cut them too short to begin with, you cannot correct the mistake.

Cheerful birdbath

Decorate your garden with an arrangement in your birdbath when you are entertaining outside. You can also place complementary arrangements on your patio and beside steps. Use pale coloured flowers if the arrangements must be visible at night.

You will need
green plastic container
prepared oasis
1 bunch lime green carnations (*Dianthus*)
4 large white chrysanths (*Chrysanthemum*)
geranium stems (*Geranium*)

Place the prepared oasis firmly in the plastic container. Begin by arranging flowers and greenery around the sides of the container. Do this in such a manner that eventually the container will be hidden. The flowers should be arranged in layers to provide definition and to create a less formal effect. Distribute the flowers evenly. When the arrangement is finished, place it in the birdbath. If you are not sure how large the arrangement needs to be, you could arrange it in the birdbath to begin with. In this way you will ensure that the green plastic container does not show.

Feminine and festive

Containers with wide mouths are sometimes misleading when it comes to the number of flowers they can hold, so you should bear this in mind when you buy or pick flowers for an arrangement.

This pot creates a soft, feminine feel for an arrangement in a guest room.

You will need

container
1 bunch chinks (*Ornithogalum*)
1 bunch Irish bells (*Molucella laevis*)
1 bunch light pink stocks (*Matthiola incana*)
1 bunch pink stocks (*Matthiola incana*)

Fill the container with water and dry the sides of the pot. Make a grid of adhesive tape. We use this method as the flowers will keep longer in water than in oasis.

The stems are relatively soft but also solid, apart from the Irish bells. The small vessels that conduct the water to the flowers can easily be damaged with pressure, for example if you were to push the stems into oasis. Arrange the flowers evenly from the middle. Ensure that you do not place the flowers too densely together. As is the case with tulips, once the buds open, the flowers 'grow' in the container and they can double in size and spread in all directions.

A basket of flowers

Cane baskets make lovely containers, especially for larger, heavier blooms as they provide a strong base and prevent your arrangement from falling over. Fill the basket with newspaper or something similar and then place a container with oasis in the basket. In this way you avoid having to make the basket watertight.

You will need
basket
green plastic plate that will fit inside
  the basket
2 blocks of oasis
greenery (dodder, *Nandina domestica*,
  Geranium, rosemary (*Rosmarinus
  officinalis*))

3 proteas (*Protea cynariodes x madiba*)

5 pincushion proteas (*Leucospermum cordifolium*)

1 bunch kolkol (*Berzelia lanuginosa*)

1 small bunch green protea (*Protea scolymocephala*)

1 bunch Inca lilies (*Alstroemeria*)

1 bunch *Bupleurum griffithii*

Fill the basket with newspaper so that it will support the plate with the oasis and the flowers. Attach the oasis to the plate with adhesive tape, but ensure that the tape does not get wet, otherwise it will not adhere. Now place the plate with the oasis in the basket.

Use dodder or ivy to disguise the plate and oasis. Begin by arranging greenery all around the edges of the basket.

Create a focal point here and there with the greenery. Arrange the flowers in groups. For example, place two large proteas together on one side, and one on the opposite side of the arrangement.

Proteas are heavy flowers, so be sure to push them into the middle of the oasis to prevent it from breaking up. Also place them relatively low in the arrangement, so that they rest on the edges of the container.

Distribute the Incas and the pincushions in the same manner.

Always ensure that there is a balance of colour and form in your arrangement. Use the natural shape of the flowers to determine their placement.

Perfect balance

Sometimes people shy away from using lovely glass containers such as this because they do not know how to keep the flowers in place without oasis, which would look ugly in clear glass. An easy solution is to place adhesive tape over the mouth of the container to form a grid.

Then finish the arrangement with ivy around the edges so that the tape does not show. A container with a wide mouth such as this one takes a surprising number of flowers. Take this into account when you are planning your arrangement.

You will need

1 bunch (10 stems) Irish bells (*Molucella laevis*)

1 bunch light purple Michaelmas daisies (*Aster novi-belgii*)

1 bunch bluegum stems (*Eucalyptus*)

5 stems large white chrysanths (*Chrysanthemum*)

1 bunch cornflowers (*Centaurea cyanus*)

ivy (*Hedera*)

Begin the arrangement by working from the outer edge inwards and distribute the plant material evenly throughout. Place the cornflowers and the chrysanths last. The cornflower stems are very delicate, so they almost depend on the blooms with thicker stems and more foliage to keep them in position.

For this arrangement I have used only a few chrysanths. I placed them right at the end to ensure that they were evenly distributed in the arrangement and create maximum impact.

Brass comeback

Do you remember how popular brass containers were in the late seventies and early eighties? Let these containers reclaim their former glory by filling them with the warm colours of bright yellow pincushions and wild saffron.

You will need
brass container
adhesive tape or oasis
10 yellow pincushions (*Leucospermum cordifolium*)
1 bunch wild saffron or safflower (*Carthamus*)
dodder

You could use oasis in the container, or a grid of adhesive tape over the mouth if you struggle to keep the flowers upright. Wind dodder around the mouth of the container to create a base and to hide the oasis or tape. Now arrange the flowers in groups, as shown in the photos. Lastly place a few more stems of dodder to hang down the sides and finish the arrangement.

Christmas tree

A wonderful idea for an unusual Christmas tree is to place dry branches with a pleasing shape in an asbestos or terracotta pot with small pebbles to secure them.

Make decorations to hang from the branches using dodder and other plant material, finished off with ribbon and crystal or pearl pins. Your Christmas tree will definitely save the day if your turkey doesn't make the grade!

You will need

container
dry branches
florist's wire
white stones and pebbles
dodder
air plant (*Tillandsia*)
crystals
pearl or crystal pinheads
ribbon

Use a relatively heavy, deep container for the tree. You can use any branches that have an interesting shape. I used *Prunus* branches stripped of foliage and fine twigs. Suspend the branches upside down to allow them to dry out. If you use them immediately, they tend to bend within a few days as they wilt. While this could also create a pleasing effect, bear it in mind. Keep the branches together by holding them upside down and binding them with florist's wire. Place the bound bunch in the pot, which you fill with pebbles from the beach or a nursery. Sometimes it is also necessary to tie individual branches to others to support them. Use silver or gold wire for this purpose.

Create decorations with dodder balls around which you have tied ribbon, silver thread and wire, thus making loops. Use pearl pins to fasten the ribbon to the balls. Add some crystals for additional bling.

You can also use air plants with the dodder. Simply thread satin ribbon through the leaves and finish off with a crystal. Use pins once again to fasten the ribbon to the plant material. Pieces of air plant can also be attached to the balls of dodder to create another interesting shape.

Advent wreath

It's time to break away from the traditional green and red that is so monotonously evident in the festive season. Why not make a festive wreath in the earthy colours of dodder and air plants with fynbos cones and sea holly? Charcoal candles finish this wreath most effectively. An Advent wreath is made at least four weeks before Christmas, so I chose plant material that would last a long time and maintain its shape once it had dried out.

You will need
ring of oasis
4 candles
air plants (*Tillandsia*)
dodder (rolled into balls like wool)
kolkol (*Berzelia lanuginosa*)
sea holly (*Eryngium maritimum*)
florist's wire

Oasis rings are available at most florist shops. Just as with blocks of oasis, the ring should absorb water naturally, and not be forced under the water.

Now the more difficult part begins. Wrap dodder around the ring. Use small pieces at a time, and wind them firmly around the oasis taking care not create too dense a covering. Make hairpins out of the florist's wire, or use real hairpins. Use these to secure the dodder. Tidy wayward bits of dodder by weaving them into the covered ring. Place the candles upright in the oasis. You can also use candle holders; these are available from most florist shops.

Start adding the air plant and arrange bits around the candles. Bear in mind the natural shape and growing pattern of the air plant as you work with it. Once again secure with the wire hairpins.

Make organic Christmas balls with the dodder by rolling it up like balls of wool. Now make a wire stem by threading the wire through the ball and twisting the two ends around one another. Place these in groups close to the candles. You can also tie the dodder balls together so that they sit firmly in the arrangement.

Complete the wreath by filling any spaces with kolkol and sea holly.

Three dimensional

This arrangement can displayed in three different three ways by placing the plastic plate on which has been made in three different outer containers. Large arrangements such as these are highly adaptable and you can change the basic container according to the occasion, the available space and the room in which it will be displayed. In this case the arrangement is literally, according to the size of the container, big, bigger, biggest...

You will need

green plastic plate that fits in the container you are using
oasis
adhesive tape
container(s)
ivy (*Hedera*)
11 proteas (*Protea cynaroides* and *P. cynaroides x madiba*)
2 bunches pincushions (*Leucospermum cordifolium*)
1 bunch small green proteas (*Protea scolymocephala*)
1 bunch *Bupleurum griffithii*
1 bunch *Brunia albiflora*
1 bunch kolkol (*Berzelia lanuginosa*)
2 bunches Safari Sunset conebush (*Leucadendron*)
dodder (rolled into tennis-ball sizes)
florist's wire to hold stems of dodder

I made holes in the plastic plate and threaded wire handles through them, to make moving the arrangement easy despite its weight. Place the oasis in the plate and fasten it with adhesive tape. This works very well as long as the tape does not get wet, so ensure that the plate is dry. Now place the plate with the attached oasis in the container you wish to use for the arrangement.

Start by arranging the ivy around the sides. Ensure that the adhesive tape, oasis and plate do not show. Now roughly form the outside edge of the arrangement so that you can work within this shape. I used the cone bush for this purpose. Before you carry on, make sure you know where the arrangement will be placed. If the arrangement is to be displayed against a wall or in a corner, it is not necessary to place flowers all the way around.

The back of the arrangement can be filled with greenery so that you can use the flowers in the front.

Arrange the biggest flowers (in this case the proteas) evenly through the arrangement. Bearing in mind the weight of the proteas, it is wise to place them quite low. I have placed three groups of proteas within the frontal globe of the arrangement.

Use the rest of the flowers in groups, filling the spaces between the proteas so that the flowers form a balanced picture. I have filled the top of the arrangement with greenery, as owing to its height the arrangement is unlikely to be viewed from the above.

I have also chosen hardier fynbos flowers (apart from the ivy and the *Bupleurum griffithii*) as they last longer. Even when they are dry, they still look attractive.